Kaizen
Primary School

Whiffy Wilson

the wolf who wouldn't wash

For Lucie – C.H
To Eddie – L.L

ORCHARD BOOKS
338 Euston Road, London NW1 3BH
Orchard Books Australia
Level 17/207 Kent Street, Sydney, NSW 2000

First published in 2011 by Orchard Books
First paperback publication in 2011
This edition published in 2012

ISBN 978 1 40830 919 3

Text © Caryl Hart 2011
Illustrations © Leonie Lord 2011

A CIP catalogue record for this book is available from the British Library.

1 3 5 7 9 10 8 6 4 2

Printed in China

Orchard Books is a division of Hachette Children's Books, an Hachette UK company.
www.hachette.co.uk

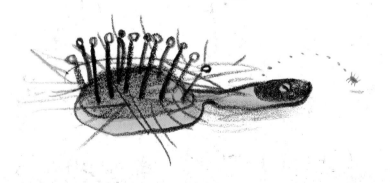

There was a wolf called Wilson
Who never brushed his hair.
He never washed his paws or face
Or changed his underwear.

His fur was full of beasties,

He had fungus on his toes,

He ate his dinner with his paws

Then wiped them on his clothes.

"HAVE A BATH!"

his mother cried,

"Or you can't go out to play."

"No way!" growled Whiffy Wilson,

And then he ran away.

Wilson grabbed his teddy bear
And hid in next-door's shed.

He found a pile of coal sacks

And made himself a bed.

"I'll be as wild as a wolf should be,
Until I'm all grown up."
Then he poked his finger up his nose –
He *was* a mucky pup!

Early in the morning,
Whiffy Wilson heard a noise . . .
It was Dotty, Wilson's favourite friend
Looking for her toys.

"Eeeeuuw! What a stink!" cried Dotty,

as she rummaged in the shed.

"EEEEEEEEEK!"

she shrieked,

"A MONSTER!
SNORING IN
ITS BED!"

"A monster?! Where?!" yelped Wilson, leaping in the air.

"It's you, you twit!" said Dotty. "You gave me such a scare!"

"I'm not a monster!" Wilson whined,
As he scratched his hairy belly,
"I'm only living here because
My mum says I'm too smelly."

"We'll soon fix that," beamed Dotty,
And she marched him down the path . . .

Up the stairs she dragged him,
And plonked him in the bath.

She poured in steaming water,
And scrubbed him with a mop.

"Get off! Let GO!" whined Wilson,
But Dotty didn't stop.

She squirted him with pink shampoo,
And rubbed it on his snout.

Then pulled a nit comb through his fur,
And scraped his ear wax out.

She cut his filthy toenails,
And rinsed out all the scum.

She brushed his stinky, rotten teeth,
And made him wash his . . .

. . . face!

"That's better," Dotty smiled at last,
Hauling Wilson out,

Then she wrapped him in a dressing gown . . .

and kissed him on the snout!

"Come on!"
she said,
"Let's play
outside . . .

... I'm making garden stew.
Grab that stick and stir it up!
Ooh, what a smelly brew!"

They made a mudslide down the hill,
They swung from tree to tree,
Till Wilson gasped, "Oh Dotty!
We're as grubby as can be!"

"Well, *this* dirt shows we're having fun.
It's GOOD dirt," Dotty said.
"We can wash the mud and grass stains off
Before we go to bed."

"The *bad* dirt is the kind of stuff
That's germy, gross and grotty.
It's those horrid germs that make you smell,
And make you ill and spotty."

"That's just perfect," Wilson beamed.
"Being mucky is all right!

As long as I can have a bath
And wash it off at night!"

So, Wilson learned the difference
Between bad dirt and the good.
He started washing twice a day,
Like every good wolf should.

His parents were delighted
And how this story ends
Is with Wilson feeling lucky
Having such a clever friend.